BUSINESS
MASTERY
FOR STARTUPS AND
SIDE HUSTLERS

Planning, launching and
running a business
on a budget

Anthony Lindsay - CeMaP, CeReR

Business Mastery for Startups and Side Hustlers

Planning, launching, and running a business on a budget

Other books in the series include:

ChatGPT Prompts for Startups and Side Hustlers

Business Networking for Startups and Side Hustlers

Anthony Lindsay, CeMaP, CeReR

Table Of Contents

Get Your Mind Right

Before we get into the meat and potatoes, let me share a few thoughts and patterns that I have recognized, which, in my view, are mindsets and behaviors that are barriers to success. I have worked with creatives and analytical people, and these things are common in both personality types.

As they say, 'facts don't care about your feelings.' What I mean by this is you cannot allow your emotions or feelings to prevent you from taking in facts. An example of this is when I talk to a business owner who refuses to accept that their business is failing based on the data and facts. They are convinced that they can keep doing (or not doing) what they are doing and get a better result. You must run a data-driven business and use the data to inform your decisions.

Another barrier is people who keep saying, either to themselves or to me, that they are not technical people; therefore, they cannot or will not dedicate the time it takes to learn a new process, platform, or app. I don't consider myself a super technical person. I am a visual learner, so I find reading instructions difficult. To overcome that, I tend to do YouTube tutorials. This allows me to rewind and slow down the instructions as many times as I need to.

The next pattern with startups and side hustlers is when they fail to realize that they must provide a product or service that, in its own right, generates value that a potential client views as something worth exchanging their money for. Just because you love your idea and you think that it is a great idea, it doesn't mean that others will. The market will decide. If you have a good product or service that people value and enough people know about it, you will make money.

Another observation which has become even more prevalent over the past few years, is people looking for what I call the virtue or pity sale. Let me explain this one in a way that I don't end up getting cancelled. As you probably know, I am not a fan of virtue signalling. This is where a business owner positions themselves or their product in a category such as 'Veteran owned,' and they expect that simply identifying as a part of that community means people should buy their product or service.

Let me be clear, there is nothing wrong with letting people know that you are a veteran in fact I encourage it, but you should not expect people to buy just because you are a veteran. You should have a superior product or service that adds value to people to the extent that they want to exchange their money for your product or service.

My younger brother Barrington is a Navy Veteran, and I honor every single person who is brave enough to fight for our country, BUT with that said, it does not obligate me to purchase his product or service. You can replace 'Veteran' with 'Woman owned,' 'Black owned,' 'Rainbow flag,' 'BLM,' 'Balding men'—just kidding about that one, but you get the message.

As you build your brand, you should certainly take into account what your community needs and what they value, but it is a form of manipulation if you feel that just because you are a minority owned, female business, I should do business with and overlook that you're not a good business.

Another mindset and pattern that I have recognized, primarily in creatives, is something that I understand but constantly rant about online. Making a logo or a song is not curing cancer. It's not ending homelessness or world hunger, so please, just get over yourself.

As AI develops and platforms such as Canva and Wix integrate more and more automation, the idea that a designer is a vital part of me building my brand becomes more and more ludicrous. I cannot see a world where, in 2026 and beyond, startups and side hustlers are paying graphic designers hundreds or thousands of dollars to create a logo or do branding.

The same goes for digital marketers and copywriters. This serves as a warning to people who think like Kodak was thinking when digital photography started to take off. Don't bury your head in the sand.

Learn to leverage the technology to make money for the few months that you have left.

Another pattern I see is when people feel that their product or service has value but they don't value the products and services of others, therefore, are reluctant to pay professionals for their services.

This book is written for people who have a limited budget. I am a huge advocate for being wise with your spending. You should save money whenever you can, but there is a huge difference between that and being cheap.

Spend money on the things that will save you time or money in the long run. I share several free or cheap platforms in this book. Don't feel that just because you can do a thing that you should do a thing. I usually see this when you have a coach or consultant who charges thousands for their course but won't pay an accountant or lawyer a few hundred dollars to make sure that the business is set up correctly or pay a web designer to build their website, which is going to get them the clients.

Value other people's service and be willing to pay others for their skill just as you expect to be paid for yours. I see this when I tell people about ChatGPT and they rant and rave about how amazing it is and how much time it saves them. Then, when I ask them if they have upgraded to the paid version, which is faster and more reliable, they scoff at the $20 per month that it costs, even though the system has already saved them time and money by replacing some paid services that they used to use.

The last thing, which links with many of the other points: **Start using AI in your business.** Stop fighting it and let it happen. You will not win the battle against the inevitable, so work with it. Learn it and use it. AI will not replace you, BUT people who learn to use AI will!

Here is a one of our GPT's specifically for Startups and Side Hustlers. This will make your life so much easier, and possible replace expensive business coaches and consultants.

Opening

It was September or October of 1991. I had accomplished a goal that I had set for myself about four years earlier. My goal was to get a record deal. One of my closest friends to this day, Sanielle, had introduced me to her boyfriend, who was A&R at an independent record label. She arranged a meeting with him so he could listen to my demo. Keep in mind, this was 1991, before the internet and in the early days of email. I had recorded a demo tape using money I had saved from working at McDonald's in the Bronx, and with the help of the money that I was supposed to have used for my high school graduation photos.

I had decided that since I was going to be famous someday, I didn't want my high school photos found by some nosy reporter trying to dig up information about the world's biggest rapper.

My rap name was 'Quiz'—I had gone through a few other names, but this one was best suited for me. I was in a rap group called 'Show and Pruve'; I was Pruve, and that was not a typo. Pruve stood for Potential Revealed Under Various Extremes. Just typing that makes me realize how old I am.

It all started about four years prior when my sister Marsha had gone to a concert in Houston featuring Run DMC. One of the performers was Joeski Love doing his hit, 'The Pee Wee Herman'. He had a dancer named KV 501. You will need to Google all of this because I know it all sounds so bizarre. Anyway, Kevin 'KV' and my sister became friends. She told him she had a brother in the Bronx who wanted to be a rapper.

It turned out that I lived not too far from Parkchester, where KV and Joe lived, which incidentally was not far from the Castle Hill projects where J Lo grew up. I thought I would add that because her life would have been very different if I had run into her on the train—LOL.

So, to keep the story moving, KV and I became friends, and he introduced me to a DJ who became my DJ. My DJ introduced me to a rapper named 'The Don', who was signed to Russell Simmons' spin-off label, Def Jam RAL. Don and I quickly became close friends. Don got me into Def Jam; I was still in high school at the time, and after school, I would head to the city and hang out with people Slick Rick, like LL Cool J, Flavor Flav, Rakim, Jay Z and the Def Jam crew. Don helped me develop my rap style.

I produced my demo consisting of a few songs, but the standout song was called 'Games', which I wrote with another friend named Omar.

When I approached labels, I kept getting told that I needed a manager, so I found one named Rocky, who took me to Boston to record a demo with my producer, Paul Romano.

Everyone was loving the project, so when I got the call saying that I had a deal, I was excited but not surprised because from the day I decided that I was going to get a deal, I pictured it every day. So, I signed my deal, started touring, and doing shows with Don, and trying to figure out how to make my marginal rap skills generate a million dollars. I quickly realized that to make real money, I would have to understand the business side of music.

This is where my journey truly starts, and this is the launchpad for this book. I will pick up the story as we get further into the book, but it's very important that you understand the journey. It's like when you hear a comedian for the first time, and everything seems perfect. The timing of every joke, the punchlines, the body movement—it didn't happen overnight.

It was a process of bombing time after time but never giving up. It's understanding what works and what doesn't. This is the journey of a successful entrepreneur. This is why the information in this book works and is evergreen. It's based on over 30 years of experience. You don't have to make the mistakes I did. Instead, you can follow this blueprint and make it happen now!

Acknowledgement

We all have people who believe in us more than we believe in ourselves. There are countless individuals who saw my potential even when I was squandering it. This book is dedicated to Sanielle, Don, KV, Gary 'Silky Don' Davis, Fran Lover, Big Lou, Carl, Urskin, Ken Francis, and John Patillo from my days as 'Quiz,' and to those who guided me as I transitioned into corporate America, where I found a whole new set of role models and mentors.

Sometimes the people who inspire us the most don't even realize the profound impact they have on our lives. A special thanks to Martin Oguzie who continues to inspire me.

I am fortunate to have a great family who has always believed in me through my ups and downs.

I feel like I am finally achieving what all these people knew I was capable of. So, for my US and UK crew, here we go—let's get that bag!

Thinking Of A Master Plan

A well-crafted business plan is the cornerstone of a successful enterprise. It serves as a comprehensive guide, articulating goals, strategies, and potential challenges with clarity and precision. It holds you accountable to yourself and to any stakeholders who engage with your vision. Unfortunately, many overlook this crucial step. The common refrain is that they have an internal roadmap, or because they aren't seeking bank loans, a business plan is unnecessary. This assumption is a critical misstep.

Consider this document a strategic ally in your entrepreneurial journey—a tool that translates your vision into actionable steps and measurable outcomes. It's vital for securing financing, as it showcases to investors or lenders a lucid growth trajectory and a pledge to responsible management. Furthermore, a business plan is a dynamic instrument for ongoing review and refinement, ensuring that your business remains agile and prosperous in a rapidly changing market.

Statistics underscore the importance of a business plan: startups with a business plan are 16% more likely to succeed than those without one. Additionally, companies that regularly review and update their business plans grow 30% faster than those that don't engage in such planning.

A business plan also serves to align your budget with your goals and provides insight into your competitive landscape. An effectively formulated business plan will aid in developing a detailed customer avatar, which is crucial for targeted marketing efforts.

Ultimately, the adage holds true: People don't plan to fail; they fail to plan. Thus, a business plan is not just a document but an essential navigator for the intricate voyage from an initial idea to becoming a market leader.

To conclude and put this into practice, a step-by-step guide to writing a business plan should include the following:

1. Executive Summary: An overview of your business and plans.

2. Company Description: What you do, who you serve, and your business goals.

3. Market Analysis: Research on your industry, market, and competitors.

4. Organization and Management: Your business and management structure.

5. Service or Product Line: Your products or services and the value they provide.

6. Marketing and Sales: Your strategy for attracting and retaining customers.

7. Funding Request: If you're seeking funding, detail your requirements.

8. Financial Projections: Provide financial forecasts to back up your funding request.

9. Appendix: An optional section with resumes, permits, or other legal documentation.

Begin by setting clear, actionable goals, and remember, your business plan is a living document—revisit and revise it regularly as your business evolves.

In essence, it is not merely a plan but an indispensable roadmap that navigates the complex journey from concept to market leader.

We recommend **LivePlan software** this will break down the process into smaller more digestible pieces and don't forget about your customer avatar.

Crafting a business plan is a strategic exercise that transforms your vision into a viable business trajectory.

By following a structured, step-by-step approach, you can develop a document that not only guides your business decisions but also communicates your vision to stakeholders. Remember, a business plan is not static; it should evolve with your business, allowing for flexibility and growth. Now, let's take these steps and embark on the journey from idea to execution.

Why not try LivePlan?

Take Action Chapter 1

Here's a SMART action plan tailored to writing a business plan:

Action: Complete a comprehensive business plan that outlines the roadmap for business growth and operations.

Specific & Measurable: Each section of the business plan will be drafted and reviewed to ensure completeness and accuracy.

Achievable: Dedicate two hours daily to writing and researching each section, starting with the executive summary, and progressing systematically through to the appendix.

Relevant: The business plan will serve as a guide for strategic decision-making and as a crucial document for potential investors.

Time-bound: The aim is to complete the draft within 30 days, with an additional two weeks allocated for revisions based on feedback.

I'm Not A Businessman, I'm A Business Man!

Jay Z said it best, I'm not a businessman and being a business, man. The former might imply a transactional existence bounded by the conventional 9-to-5 constraints, while the latter represents a paradigm shift—a declaration that you, in your entirety, embody the enterprise you've brought to life. It's about embracing the identity of your business, living, and breathing your brand, and aligning your personal values with your professional endeavors. You are the brand, so it should be congruent.

This chapter isn't just about business strategies; it's about personal transformation and the symbiotic relationship between the entrepreneur and their creation.

You cannot have a million dollar idea with a part-time work ethic. You have to be willing to do the things that others will not do to reach your goals. This might mean waking up at 3am to work on your idea, or staying in the office when everyone else has left. This is the spirit of a true startup or side hustler.

Empire State Of Mind

Regardless of whether you have a startup or a side hustle, having your paperwork in order is essential.

You need to choose the correct business formation for your short and long-term goals. I always advise clients to speak with either an accountant or a lawyer. Yes, it will cost some money, and yes, you could do it yourself, but never be too frugal to pay professionals who can provide the best advice and potentially save you money in the long run.

Here are the key business formation options along with their pros and cons:

1. Sole Proprietorship:

- Pros: Simplest and least expensive option to establish, complete control by the owner, and minimal regulatory burden.

- Cons: The owner is personally liable for all business debts, it can be harder to raise capital, and it may be perceived as a less professional entity.

2. Partnership:

- Pros: Easy to establish with minimal formalities, profits are shared and taxed on a personal level, and it benefits from combined skills and resources.

- Cons: Partners are jointly and individually liable for business debts, and disputes can arise over decisions and profit sharing.

3. Limited Liability Company (LLC):

- Pros: Limited liability for owners, flexible profit distribution, and no double taxation.

- Cons: More complex to set up than a sole proprietorship or partnership, higher startup costs, and possible additional state taxes.

4. Corporation (C-Corp):

- Pros: Limited liability, unlimited potential for growth through the sale of stock, and perpetual existence.

- Cons: More expensive to establish, subject to double taxation, and more regulatory requirements.

5. S Corporation (S-Corp):

- Pros: Tax benefits—profits and some losses are taxed on personal income tax, not subject to double taxation, and limited liability protection.

- Cons: Stricter operational processes, limits on the number of shareholders, and more scrutiny from the IRS.

6. B Corporation:

- Pros: Can make a profit while focusing on social good, potentially more attractive to a certain customer base, and employee engagement.

- Cons: Must meet high standards of social and environmental performance, accountability, and transparency; possibly more costly to maintain.

Each business formation has its nuances, and the choice depends on individual circumstances. For example, according to the Small Business Administration, over 70% of US businesses are owned and operated by sole proprietors, primarily due to the simplicity of the structure. However, Forbes reports that LLCs are becoming increasingly popular due to their flexibility and the protection of personal assets.

If you need assistance or guidance visit www.astorbusinesscenters.com

A thoughtful approach to selecting your business structure is a foundational step in your entrepreneurial journey. It is a decision that should not be made lightly. I always advise my clients to speak to a lawyer or accountant for professional support.

Once chosen, it will shape everything from your liability to your tax payments, to how much paperwork you'll need to do. Here's a step-by-step guide to make this decision:

1. Define your business goals and assess your needs.

2. Research each business structure and consult with a professional.

3. Consider the potential for growth and the need to attract investors.

4. Evaluate your willingness to deal with administrative paperwork and formalities.

5. Make an informed decision based on long-term strategic planning for your business.

Take Action Chapter 2

Focusing on the foundational aspects of business structure and legality, a SMART action plan could be:

Specific: Research and decide on the most suitable business formation for your startup or side hustle.

Measurable: Obtain a clear understanding of the advantages and limitations of each business structure, including sole proprietorship, partnership, LLC, C-Corp, S-Corp, and B-Corp.

Achievable: Schedule consultations with a business lawyer and an accountant to discuss the implications of each structure for your specific business goals and financial situation.

Relevant: Ensure that the chosen business structure aligns with your current needs and future growth plans, taking into consideration factors like liability, taxes, and investment needs.

Time-bound: Aim to finalize the decision on your business structure within the next 30 days to maintain momentum in setting up your business operations.

All Eyez On Me

Branding is an area that is near and dear to my heart for several reasons. Firstly, I used to own a graphic design business.

As my rap career developed, I realized that I couldn't afford to pay others for typesetting. These were the early days when design software was prohibitively expensive. Fortunately, at the time, I was working part-time at Kinko's, which is now FedEx Kinko's. One of the many perks was access to software and copy machines. I know it was wrong, but I used to pay the night shift manager to run copies of my flyers.

That manager was earning more from his side hustle than from his full-time job. We got to the point where we started doing flyers for Caroline's Comedy Club, the Latin Quarter, and for too many DJs and promoters to mention. During this time, I perfected (if that's what you call it) my design style.

Using software like Quark, I realized how vital logos are to people. Who would have known that I'd end up married to a graphic designer? My wife is an exceptional designer, so I hope she doesn't read this chapter. The truth is a logo is just a logo. Don't get hung up on it and delay your entire project trying to find the perfect logo; but here's where I contradict myself: Branding is very important, so you should take the time to think it through. You can find people in the gig economy to do your branding, but make sure they know their stuff. You don't want to end up like the Chevy Nova.

The importance of consistent branding cannot be overstated. It's the visual and verbal language that tells your story and sets the tone for your customer's experience. Consider the cautionary tale of the Chevy Nova. In Spanish, "no va" translates to "doesn't go," which is a less-than-ideal name for a car. This oversight highlights the significance of understanding your ideal client and the context in which your brand will be received. A brand extends far beyond a logo or a name; it encompasses everything from your color scheme to your mission statement, resonating with your audience's values and lifestyle. It's about creating a cohesive identity that customers can trust, relate to, and advocate for.

Take the time to build your brand with intention, so it can effectively represent your business and resonate with your audience across different cultures, print methods and contexts.

Take Action Chapter 3

A SMART action plan might include the following components:

Specific: Develop a cohesive branding strategy that reflects the company's values, mission, and appeals to the target audience.

Measurable: Create brand guidelines that include logo usage, color palette, typography, voice, and tone.

Achievable: Collaborate with a branding professional or use online design tools to refine your brand's visual and verbal identity.

Relevant: Ensure the branding resonates with your target demographic and stands out in the competitive landscape.

Time-bound: Set a goal to complete the branding strategy and start implementation within the next two months.

Just like Tupac's enduring legacy through his unique style and message, "All Eyez on Me" should serve as a mantra for your branding efforts. Your brand is the face of your business and the promise to your customers.

With a clear, distinctive, and consistent brand strategy, you will capture the attention of your ideal client, just as a legendary artist captures the hearts of fans. Remember, your brand is not just what you sell—it's the story you tell.

A few platforms where you can get branding and design support are:

www.fiverr.com

www.upwork.com

www.kudaflow.com

Another option is to use a DIY platform. Here are a few good ones:

www.canva.com

www.pixelied.com

If you are looking for graphic design or web design consider:

www.websitecasa.com

www.tinydesigns.us

www.yesiprint.com

When you know who your ideal client is, you can speak to them, and it will resonate. Your ideal client should be someone you enjoy working with, who values your product or service, and is profitable. This way, when they refer people, they will refer other quality clients because birds of a feather flock together. And by the way, avoid Gumtree. I was once told that Gumtree is where cheap people find cheap services.

According to HBR, increasing customer retention rates by 5% increases profits by 25% to 95%. This statistic highlights the importance of focusing on the right customers. Creating a customer avatar isn't just about targeting sales; it's about building relationships.

Here's a step-by-step guide to creating your customer avatar:

1. Demographic Information: Start with the basics like age, gender, occupation, income level, education, and marital status.

2. Psychographics: Understand their values, interests, lifestyle, and challenges.

3. Behavioral Traits: Identify their buying habits, brand interactions, and product usage patterns.

4. Goals and Aspirations: Determine what they are striving to achieve, personally and professionally.

5. Pain Points: What problems do they need to solve? What keeps them up at night?

6. Sources of Information: Where do they get their information? Which social media platforms do they frequent, and who do they trust?

7. Objections: What might prevent them from purchasing your product or service?

8. Role in the Purchase Process: Are they the decision-maker or an influencer?

9. Segmentation: Group similar avatars to target marketing efforts effectively.

10. Validation: Test your avatar with real potential customers to ensure accuracy.

Establishing a solid legal and structural foundation for your business is as vital as any marketing or sales strategy. It defines the framework within which your business will operate and grow.

With a clear, well-informed decision on your business formation, supported by professional advice, you will set the stage for a startup or side hustle that's built to last, just like the enduring Empire State.

Take action now to build your empire with confidence and clarity.

Made You Look: Identifying Your Target Audience

Hopefully, you will gain a lot of practical information from this book, but if there's only one takeaway, let it be this: If you try to please everyone, you will please no one. Having a very specific, well-documented, and detailed customer avatar, or ideal client, is vital. A well-thought-out, well-developed customer avatar will inform everything that you do—your logo, your marketing, your fonts, your networking, your social media, everything. This is why it is so important to get it right.

When I first started rapping, I tried to sound like whoever was popular on the radio (yes, I said radio). I went through my Special Ed phase, then Rakim, and then I tried to sound like Don. What I ended up with was a hot mess. I couldn't find an audience. I wasn't good-looking enough to be Special Ed, who, by the way, never showed up for a concert that I booked him for. I wasn't skilled enough to sound like Rakim, not to mention I didn't have the voice, and Don was himself. What I learned is that I needed to focus and find my audience. This is how I ended up being me and making music for my particular audience.

Remember, your ideal client avatar is a living profile that evolves as you learn more about your market. Revisit and refine it regularly to ensure your marketing efforts are as effective as possible. By understanding and connecting with your ideal client, you're more likely to build a loyal customer base and, ultimately, a more successful business.

SMART action plan could be as follows:

Specific: Create a comprehensive customer avatar to guide all marketing and product development efforts.

Measurable: The customer avatar should include demographic details, psychographics, behavior patterns, goals, pain points, preferred media channels, and potential objections.

Achievable: Use market research, customer surveys, and existing data from your business to inform the customer avatar.

Relevant: Ensure the avatar accurately reflects the segment of the market most likely to purchase your products or services and aligns with your brand values.

Time-bound: Aim to complete the customer avatar within the next 4 weeks to begin tailoring your marketing strategies accordingly.

By understanding precisely who your ideal client is, you can create targeted messages that resonate deeply, foster loyalty, and drive sales.

Just as a musician finds their unique sound to captivate their audience, so too must your business find its voice to captivate your ideal clients.

Don't let your message fade into the background noise of the market. Make them look, make them listen, and make them remember with a brand that speaks directly to their needs and desires.

The Takeover: Partnering with Power Players

So, there I was, 19 years old with a record deal. What do I do now? How do I connect with the right people? I was signed to an independent record label with limited distribution, and this was well before the internet revolutionized music distribution. And, because of my hubris, I arrogantly turned down a counteroffer from another indie label, which later ended up producing some big names. Stupid, stupid, stupid, but I digress.

I realized that I had to network with the big names, so I started attending all of the industry parties. I was at the screening of 'Juice,' one of the first significant hip-hop movies, around the same time that Don had done a song on the soundtrack for a movie called 'Livin' Large.' I went to all the significant music conventions of the time—'Jack the Rapper,' 'How Can I Be Down,' 'The Vibe Music Conference,' and many more. I made sure I knew who the big players were and kept my name out there.

As a startup or side hustler in 2024 and beyond, you have tools that I didn't have. You can use LinkedIn and other social media platforms. The key is to generate a list of the top 50 people in your niche and engage with them online strategically. A report from Influencer Marketing Hub states that influencer marketing is set to grow to approximately $13.8 billion in 2021. The right connections can make a significant difference. Like, comment, and share their posts, but do so authentically.

When it comes to resilience and dealing with rejection, remember: "no" doesn't mean "never." It may simply mean "not now." Forbes suggests that 73% of salespeople give up after one or two no's, but 80% of prospects say no at least four times before they say yes. Keep this in mind when you first approach your list of influencers.

Here are some practical steps to connect with those top 50 influencers:

1. Research and identify the top 50 influencers in your niche using tools like BuzzSumo, Followerwonk, or LinkedIn's search function.

2. Engage with their content in a meaningful way; don't just like their posts—leave thoughtful comments and share with insights that add value.

3. Build a rapport by consistently engaging with their content over time. Don't just reach out cold and ask for something.

4. When the time is right, reach out with a personalized message that shows you understand their work and have been an active member of their audience.

5. Be prepared for rejection, but also be ready to persist. If you receive a no, be gracious, and ask if you can check back in after some time or if there's someone else, they recommend you talk to.

6. If an influencer responds positively, have a clear and concise proposal ready that outlines what you're asking and what you can offer in return.

Remember, building these relationships is about long-term engagement. It's not just about what these influencers can do for you, but also about how you can contribute to their community. Be patient, be persistent, and most importantly, be genuine.

By using these strategies, you'll not only amplify your visibility but also potentially tap into vast pools of followers, peeling off some to become your customers. This will not happen overnight; you will need to be persistent and consistent. It might take years, but you must keep pushing.

Take Action Chapter 4

The SMART action plan for identifying and connecting with the top 50 influencers in your niche could be:

Specific: Research and create a list of the top 50 influencers within your niche who have the reach and authority to amplify your message.

Measurable: Measure engagement with these influencers through likes, comments, and shares on their posts, and track responses to direct outreach efforts.

Achievable: Develop a strategy for regular engagement with these influencers' content. Create genuine and thoughtful interactions before reaching out directly with a personalized proposal.

Relevant: Ensure the influencers are aligned with your brand values and have an audience that overlaps with your target customer base.

Time-bound: Aim to establish a connection with all 50 influencers within three months, with a goal to have at least 10% actively engaging with your content or collaborating in some form.

Embarking on "The Takeover" isn't just about getting noticed; it's about forming strategic partnerships that can elevate your brand to new heights. By focusing on building relationships with key influencers, you tap into a reservoir of potential customers and advocates.

Remember, resilience is key; a 'no' today might turn into a 'yes' tomorrow, so keep the conversation going and maintain a presence that's hard to overlook.

I Need Love

There are approximately 7.8 billion people on the planet, yet no two individuals are exactly alike. Despite this incredible diversity, research has broadly categorized the reasons for consumer purchases into three main areas: health, wealth, and relationships.

When you have a deep understanding of these motivations and a clear picture of your ideal client, you can craft a message that resonates deeply. Further, if you consider the two key drivers for purchasing decisions—moving away from pain or moving toward pleasure—you can create a message that converts at a high rate.

According to a study published in the "Journal of Consumer Psychology," the motivation to resolve cognitive dissonance, which is the mental discomfort of having conflicting beliefs or behaviors, can be a powerful driver in purchasing decisions, particularly in the health sector. For example, a person who values health but eats poorly may be compelled to purchase healthy foods or a gym membership to alleviate this dissonance. This is especially true at the beginning of the year when people look to make a fresh start.

In terms of wealth, a report by American Express found that 72% of consumers say that spending money on experiences—such as travel, dining, and entertainment—makes them happier than buying physical items, suggesting that the pursuit of pleasure plays a significant role in spending decisions related to wealth.

Regarding relationships, the psychology of gift-giving, as outlined by the "Journal of Experimental Social Psychology," indicates that people often purchase gifts to strengthen relationships and to experience the pleasure of making others happy, as well as to avoid the pain of social disapproval. Giving a small gift can help build relationships. The gift doesn't even have to cost anything. I frequently "gift" people information by sharing the name of a good business related book or website. This small gesture can have huge rewards, and even it if doesn't it's still a nice thing to do.

Here's my gift to you, it's a link to one of my favorite websites. It's where I get most of my business software. Some are free, some are cheap, most of them have lifetime offers so you won't have to pay monthly for subscriptions.

Take Action Chapter 5

Now, for creating a SMART action plan for this chapter:

Specific: Understand the psychological factors of buying based on health, wealth, and relationships and how they relate to the pursuit of pleasure or the avoidance of pain.

Measurable: Incorporate statistics and psychological research that validate these buying motivations.

Achievable: Compile examples and case studies that demonstrate how businesses can leverage these insights to craft compelling messages and offers.

Relevant: Relate these psychological principles directly to the strategies employed by startups and side hustlers, emphasizing practical applications.

Time-bound: Aim to integrate this research and finalize the chapter within six weeks, ensuring that the content is both current and applicable.

By tapping into the commonalities of human desire for health, wealth, and meaningful relationships, and the intrinsic drive to avoid pain or gain pleasure, you can tailor your business strategies to meet these fundamental needs.

Understanding these principles isn't just about influencing buying behavior; it's about connecting with the core of human experience and providing solutions that enhance lives.

Your customer avatar will help with this process. Having a clear understanding of who your ideal customer is will help you craft a message that resonates with their desires.

Have I mentioned how important and client avatar is??? If you haven't already started on yours, don't read another page until you do. Templates are available at www.anthony-lindsay.com on our 'resources' page.

Grindin': Mastering The Search Game

We are incredibly fortunate today to have the internet, ChatGPT, and other tools to find the information we need. When I was in the process of making my demo, I also had to figure out how to get it to the right person at the record label. Let me remind you again, this was before Google. I had no choice but to put in the work.

This was the late '80s when vinyl records and cassette tapes were still prevalent, and CDs were just beginning to emerge. So, I would go to record stores with a notepad and pen and rifle through the sleeves, searching for the addresses and phone numbers of the labels. I compiled a list and started sending out my demo tape (yes, a cassette tape). A few weeks later, I would receive a well-crafted, nicely worded letter telling me that the label does not accept unsolicited music.

The magic was in the signature because it was usually signed by the A&R person. I took this information and compiled a list of every record label and then started selling that list to other rappers and aspiring artists.

Nowadays, you can just Google. When people are looking for a product or service, they either search directly for the product or they might browse within a specific interest. Broadly speaking, there are two approaches: search-based and interest-based.

A report by Moz indicates that search is the number one driver of traffic to content sites, beating social media by more than 300%. As a startup or side hustler, your job is to figure out how your ideal customer searches and what their interests are, so that you can be there first. You should be present in those places so that you can be found. This is why having a website is so important. I am not saying to have a website instead of social media. I am saying in addition to it.

Having a website is crucial for various reasons. Firstly, always remember you are renting space on social media; you don't own the traffic and could be locked out at any time. I've seen it happen. According to a survey by Verisign, 84% of consumers believe that having a website makes your business more credible than just a social media page.

Secondly, in order to build effective sales funnels and employ some of the other techniques, it's easier if you have a domain name and hosting to link the apps and platforms to. Lastly, your customers expect you to have a website. It doesn't have to be extensive, but it should provide the key details.

This section not only emphasizes the value of search and interest-based discovery but also the importance of owning your platform, a lesson just as crucial in the '80s as it is in the digital age.

Getting a website up and running is easier than ever. Companies like Wix and Squarespace are built for people with little or no technical knowledge. These platforms tend to be drag and drop.

My only concern with these platforms is that just like using social media profiles, you don't own the site. You are essentially renting your business. If you are going to use one of these platforms, be sure to export the data regularly so that you have it just in case you ever get locked out.

When you transfer the data to your database or CRM you own it. The traffic is now yours. Alternatively you have traffic that you control by purchasing ads. Lastly you can earn traffic by partnering with other people. This is a great way to build your fan base and turn them into followers and then customers.

Get Money: Websites That Hustle For You

Your website should not merely be a glorified online brochure. Instead, you ought to treat your website like an employee. This means keeping it updated, maintaining clear communication, providing the necessary training, and expecting it to generate revenue, offer customer service, provide data, and show up every day. One of my ventures is a web design company named Websitecasa. We build WordPress websites in 10 business days or less, starting at $595. Interestingly, 80% of my new business conversations begin with, "I need you to rebuild my website; my old one went down, and the previous web designer wants to overcharge me to get it back up." My first question usually is, "How long has it been down?" The most common reply is, "I don't know."

This is because many people simply have a website as just this thing they own. That approach is entirely wrong. Your website should be your homepage —set it as the default when you open your browser, so you'll know immediately if and when it goes down. It should be an integral part of your sales, service, and accounting processes. It should be linked to some kind of CRM so that you are constantly gathering data. We have a product called WC Portal, which is designed for startups.

Take Action Chapter 6

Now, for the SMART action plan for this chapter:

Specific: Revamp your website to function as a proactive member of your team, contributing to sales, customer service, and data analytics.

Measurable: Use analytics to track visitor behavior, conversion rates, and customer interactions, ensuring your website is actively engaging visitors.

Achievable: Implement tools like CRM integration and active monitoring to keep your website performing its roles effectively.

Relevant: Ensure that every aspect of your website is optimized to contribute to your business goals, such as lead generation, customer retention, and revenue growth.

Time-bound: Set a deadline for the website overhaul and integration with CRM tools, aiming for completion within the next quarter.

Transform your website into an active, revenue-generating team member, and start leveraging your online presence to its fullest potential.

Treat your website not just as a static representation of your business, but as a dynamic, essential part of your daily operations and long-term strategy. With the right set-up and maintenance, your website will become the most reliable 'employee' you've ever had.

A reliable well built website can be a game changer. Waking up and checking your inbox and finding orders or sales is exciting. The more you get from your website, the more you will use it. The less you will see it as just another business expense.

One of my top tips is to send links to your website to customers who have inquired about a product or service. Answer the question and follow-up with the link to your website or the answer to their question if you happen to have an FAQ page.

Flow Like a Pro: The Rhythm Of Sales Funnels

Sales funnels are truly one of my favorite topics and could be a book in themselves. They are the engine of your sales machine, and mastering sales funnels can transform your business forever.

Having a website is just the foundation; once you start to understand sales funnels, you'll be able to turn your website into a money printing machine. Of course, I don't mean that literally, as that would be illegal. However, when you master the structure of the item, bump, one-time-only offer, cart abandonment strategy, and urgency, you will absolutely crush it. These elements work together to increase conversion rates, the average sale amount, and return on ad spend.

You have likely experienced this as a customer. It's that process when you go to buy one product, but by the time you reach the checkout, you have three. You intended to spend $30, but you end up spending $55. Or you decide not to purchase, close your browser window, and then, 10 minutes later, receive an email offering a coupon or discount for the product. These are all functions of a sales funnel.

According to Forbes, companies that have optimized their sales funnels can achieve a growth rate of 18% more than companies that don't. And, as reported by HubSpot, a well-designed sales funnel can lead to a conversion rate improvement of up to 300%. You are in someone's sales funnel right now; it's time for you to build your own.

By understanding the flow of a sales funnel, you can create a systematic, customer-focused journey that not only guides potential customers through the stages of becoming aware of, considering, and deciding to purchase your products but also keeps them coming back.

One of the great things about sales funnels is that they work for physical and virtual businesses.

Here's a basic overview of a sales funnel.

1. Sales Funnel Bump (also known as an order bump):

- This is an offer presented to customers at the checkout before they complete their purchase. It's usually a low-cost add-on to the main product they're buying. It's called a "bump" because it's designed to increase the average order value by enticing customers with an additional product or service that complements their purchase. An example could be offering batteries with an electronic device.

2. One-Time Offer (OTO):

- A one-time offer is a special deal presented to customers immediately after they've made a purchase or sometimes while they are in the process of checking out. This offer is usually heavily discounted and is available only in that moment, encouraging an impulse buy. For example, after purchasing a course, you might get offered a one-time deal on personalized coaching.

3. Cart Abandonment Strategy:

- This involves reaching out to potential customers who added items to their shopping cart but did not complete the purchase. Various methods are used to entice these customers to return and complete their purchase, such as sending follow-up emails with a reminder of the items left in the cart, offering a discount, or addressing potential objections they might have had.

4. Time-Sensitive Offer:

- A time-sensitive offer is a discount or special deal available for a limited time. The scarcity and urgency of the deal prompt customers to make a purchase decision quickly to take advantage of the offer. An example is a 24-hour flash sale on a website, which encourages immediate action.

One of the beauties of the bump and the OTO is that even if the customer doesn't take the offer, you still have the original sale item.

Each of these elements plays a crucial role in optimizing a sales funnel for better conversion rates and increased customer value. They are designed to work together to not only guide potential customers through the buying process but also to maximize the revenue from each customer interaction.

An important part of a sales funnel strategy is low friction this means that the process should flow smoothly and not require too much information from the customer or require them to enter their payment details more than once.

If you would like to know more about sales funnels, we have more information and some examples at www.startupsandsidehustlers.com

Mo Money: Sales Pages That Sell

Having a well-crafted sales page on your website for your top-selling item is pivotal in converting visitors into customers. When you funnel traffic from social media or other advertising platforms to your site, directing them to a specific sales page helps maintain their focus and increases the chances of conversion.

This page should be solely dedicated to the advertised product with a clear and compelling explanation, accompanied by an irresistible 'Buy Now' button. The goal is to streamline the customer's journey from interest to purchase without the distractions of other products or offers.

Statistics show that a focused landing page can increase conversion rates by over 55% compared to sending traffic to a general home page. Furthermore, businesses with 30 or more landing pages generate 7 times more leads than those with fewer than 10. This demonstrates the effectiveness of targeted sales pages in capturing and converting leads.

However, it's not just about the initial click or conversion. Implementing a sales funnel that begins with the sales page can further enhance the customer's journey.

By offering additional value through upsells, cross-sells, and related products after the initial purchase, you can significantly increase the average order value (AOV). For instance, companies see an average increase of 10-30% in AOV when using upselling techniques on their sales pages.

Work it

Before I forget, let me introduce you to a straightforward method to monetize your website through affiliate marketing. Think of this as establishing an "off-ramp" - a paid pathway that you create for visitors who may not be purchasing your services directly.

For example, on my web design page, I've set up off-ramps. When some visitors decide to build their own site, I offer affiliate links to Do-It-Yourself (DIY) web builders. If a visitor clicks on one of these links and subscribes to the DIY platform, I earn a commission. I apply a similar strategy on my finance-related websites. The key is to select products or services that complement what you offer and integrate affiliate links on your site. This can generate passive income where a direct sale might not have been possible.

Affiliate marketing can also be pursued as a standalone side hustle. It's perplexing why so many business owners overlook the potential to leverage their website's real estate effectively. A top site for finding affiliate programs is CJ.com, among many others. Typically, you can spot affiliate opportunities at the footer of a company's website.

Affiliate marketing is a business model where you earn income by promoting other companies' products or services on your website. When someone clicks on the affiliate links placed on your site and makes a purchase, you receive a commission. It's a win-win: companies get more sales, and you earn from your recommendations without having to provide the product or service yourself.

When selecting an affiliate program, it's advantageous to opt for those offering recurring billing over one-time payouts, though both have their merits. I have a preference for recurring billing as it can provide a steady income stream. Look for "sticky" products or services, such as SaaS (Software as a Service) offerings. A sticky product is one that customers continue to use over time.

Business software is an excellent example, as companies tend to remain with the same software once they've integrated it into their operations. If you're comfortable with a one-time payout, you might want to consider programs like Anytime Mailbox and Opus Virtual Offices, both of which offer substantial commissions.

Banking products often come with the highest commissions, although they may present more challenges in terms of approval. Another key feature to look for in an affiliate program is an extended cookie duration. A long cookie life means that if a potential client clicks on your link but doesn't make an immediate purchase, you can still earn credit for the referral over a longer period. While many programs offer a 15-day cookie lifespan, I've worked with companies that provide up to a 30-day period.

It's also worth noting the option of incorporating Google ads onto your website. You simply embed the provided code into your site's HTML. Subsequently, you earn revenue every time someone clicks on one of these ads. Comparatively, Amazon offers an affiliate program where you place ads or links for Amazon products on your site, and if someone clicks through and makes a purchase, you receive a percentage of the sale.

The primary difference between Google ads and Amazon affiliate ads is the revenue model. Google ads are typically pay-per-click (PPC), meaning you get paid for each ad click regardless of whether it leads to a sale.

In contrast, Amazon's affiliate program is commission-based, paying out only when clicks result in a purchase. Choosing between the two depends on your site's traffic and audience. Google ads can provide consistent income from high-traffic sites even if visitors are not purchasing. Meanwhile, Amazon affiliate links may yield higher earnings per transaction if your audience is inclined to buy products related to your content.

Take Action Chapter 8

A SMART action plan regarding sales pages and funnels:

Specific: Create a dedicated sales page for your top-selling item with a clear 'Buy Now' option and a subsequent sales funnel.

Measurable: Track the conversion rate of the sales page and the average order value from the sales funnel.

Achievable: Utilize web design and funnel-building tools to construct the sales page and funnel sequence.

Relevant: Ensure that the sales page and funnel are aligned with the advertised product and overall business strategy.

Time-bound: Aim to launch the sales page and funnel within a set timeframe, such as 4 weeks, and evaluate performance after a further 4 weeks to make necessary adjustments.

Not Gonna Be Able To Do It

Buyer objections are a natural part of the sales process. Whether based on emotion, logic, or fear, these objections are the customer's way of expressing uncertainty or hesitation before making a purchase. Understanding and addressing these objections is critical to closing sales and building customer trust.

Emotion-based objections might arise from a customer's personal preference or discomfort with change. They might say, "I just don't feel like this product is for me." To handle this, you can employ empathy and storytelling. Use the "feel, felt, found" technique:

- Feel: "I understand how you feel..."

- Felt: "...others felt the same way..."

- Found: "...until they found how our product improved their situation."

Logic-based objections involve the customer's reasoning about the product, often around price, features, or necessity. For instance, if a customer says, "I don't see why I should pay this much when I can get something similar for less," a good strategy is to differentiate your product by highlighting its unique value proposition and return on investment.

Fear-based objections typically stem from a fear of making the wrong decision. A customer might worry about the product not delivering as promised. In this case, offering a risk-reversal, such as a money-back guarantee or a free trial, can alleviate their concerns.

Each objection is an opportunity to deepen the conversation with the customer and demonstrate the value of your offering. It's essential to listen actively, validate their concerns, and present solutions that align with their needs and goals.

By effectively addressing objections, you not only clear the path to a sale but also reinforce a positive and supportive customer relationship.

By mastering objection handling, you transform potential barriers into bridges towards closing a sale. The 'Not Gonna Be Able to Do It' chapter will guide you through turning 'no's' into 'yes's' and hesitations into affirmations, strengthening your sales approach and boosting your conversion rates. Remember, every objection is an opportunity to provide clarity and value, drawing your customer closer to a confident purchase.

Take Action Chapter 7

Here's a SMART action plan:

Specific: Develop skills to effectively address and overcome buyer objections by understanding the underlying reasons—emotion, logic, or fear.

Measurable: Aim to reduce the number of lost sales due to objections by 25% by implementing these techniques.

Achievable: Train yourself and your sales team on the 'feel, felt, found' method and other objection-handling strategies. Role-play common scenarios where objections are raised and practice responding in a way that aligns with your product's value proposition.

Relevant: Make sure that these strategies are aligned with the types of objections most commonly encountered in your industry and by your sales team.

Time-bound: Set a goal to have the training and initial practice sessions completed within one month, with regular refreshers every quarter.

Once Upon A Time Not Long Ago: Using Stories, Hooks, and Offers.

I've trained hundreds, if not thousands, of salespeople, and the most successful ones have been those who could truly understand the client's needs, fears, and buying personality. Some people make a purchase quickly and then go home and regret it, while others take a long time to be convinced. It is commonly said that most people buy on emotion and then justify the purchase with logic.

This is evident in car advertisements, where you often see a person driving in the mountains with a beautiful companion and a dog, then sitting by a campfire, and later running by the beach. If we bought solely based on logic, a simple image of the car with its specifications would suffice.

As a salesperson, it's crucial to pre-emptively address objections. One effective way to do this is by engaging them with a compelling headline (the hook), drawing them in with a relatable narrative (the story), and finally presenting them with an irresistible proposition (the offer).

Statistics from the Harvard Business Review suggest that emotional connectivity is a key predictor of customer behavior and brand loyalty. For example, brands that optimize their customer engagement can outperform competitors by 85% in sales growth.

Here's how the process works:

- **The Hook**: Start with a powerful headline or question that addresses a key pain point or dream scenario for your customer. For example, "Imagine doubling your business revenue in just 3 months..."
- **The Story**: Weave a narrative that relates to the hook, illustrating the transformation or solution your product or service provides. For example, "John Doe was struggling to keep his business afloat until he discovered our game-changing marketing strategy..."
- **The Offer**: Present your product or service as the solution, with clear benefits and a call to action. Make sure it feels exclusive and time-sensitive to create urgency. For example, "Join the elite group of entrepreneurs who have transformed their businesses with our strategy. Act now and receive an exclusive bonus available only for the next 48 hours!"

By using this structure, you align the emotional desire with logical reasoning, making it a potent formula for compelling sales pitches that are difficult for customers to refuse.

When crafting your sales pitch, always remember to tailor the hook, story, and offer to your audience, ensuring relevance and increasing the likelihood of conversion.

Touch The Sky: Networking To New Heights

In my book 'Business Networking for Startups and Side Hustlers,' I delve into the nuances of business networking and offer, if I may say so myself, some exceptional strategies. The cornerstone of effective business networking is having a strategic plan.

The most common pitfall I observe with startups and side hustlers is that they fail to integrate networking into their business strategy. They don't "dig their well before they're thirsty." Instead, they resort to networking only when in dire need or solely connect with individuals who can provide immediate benefits. This is fundamentally the wrong approach.

According to a survey by HubSpot, 85% of professionals consider networking to be important to career success, and yet, many don't network until it's necessary. Furthermore, LinkedIn states that 80% of professionals attribute their career advancement to networking. This illustrates the critical nature of building networks consistently, not just when you need something.

One of my dearest friends, who's made a significant impact in the music industry, is Gary "Silky Don" Davis. With a name like that, you can bet he's a force to be reckoned with. To me, he's just Silky, and he still calls me Quiz to this day.

The story of how I met Silky connects several dots in my life's journey. I was visiting the world-famous Fran Lover in East New York. Fran was collaborating with Daddy O from the rap group Stetsasonic, who was, if I recall correctly, the head of A&R for MCA Records at the time. Leaving Fran's house and walking down a street in Brooklyn on a glorious summer day, I witnessed an attractive lady stepping into what could only be described as the largest pile of dog poop I had ever seen.

Our eyes met at that unfortunate moment, and amid the awkwardness, I, being the gentleman I am, helped her clean her shoe.

We ended up on the same train, where I learned she was a singer named Charrise Arrington, signed to MCA Records. We exchanged numbers, and one thing led to another—I eventually met her manager, Silky.

This stroll down memory lane underscores a vital point: the outcomes of a conversation can be unpredictable. Don't just focus on what you can extract from others. As a business owner, you need to consistently widen your network. Attend networking events regularly, come prepared with business cards, and strive to connect on a genuine level. Ask what you can do for them and who in your network might benefit them. The laws of reciprocation are indeed powerful.

My top tip is to share a book or app that you find useful—something to make you memorable beyond just another salesperson. And for those looking to truly master networking, consider reading my book on the subject.

Remember, networking is about cultivating relationships that can bear fruit over time. It's a mutual exchange of value that often leads to opportunities and growth for all parties involved.

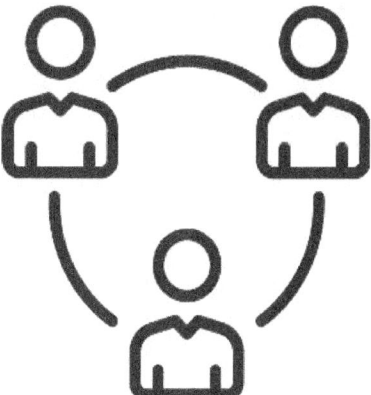

Take Action Chapter 8

Here's a SMART action plan for the chapter on networking:

Specific: Develop a networking strategy that aims to expand your professional connections within your industry and related fields.

Measurable: Set a goal to attend a certain number of networking events each quarter and to connect with a specific number of new contacts at each event.

Achievable: Research and identify networking events, both virtual and in-person, that are most likely to be attended by key players in your industry. Use platforms like LinkedIn for outreach and connection before and after events.

Relevant: Ensure that the networking events and platforms you choose are frequented by professionals and decision-makers relevant to your business goals and can provide mutual value.

Time-bound: Within the next six months, aim to have established a routine of regular networking and to have grown your network by a certain percentage, with a focus on quality connections that align with your business strategy.

Networking is not just about collecting business cards; it's about weaving a tapestry of relationships that support and enhance your business journey.

By setting clear goals and being proactive and genuine in your networking efforts, you create a web of connections that can lead to new opportunities, insights, and growth.

Like any good relationship, the connections you make through networking require nurturing to develop into strong, productive partnerships.

So set out to be memorable, be helpful, and watch as your network becomes a driving force behind your business's success.

If you want to know how to network better and find great networks where you live, checkout ' Business Networking for Startups and Side Hustlers'.

All I Do Is Win: Strategy For Success

I've talked about my music career extensively in this book which is usual because I usually draw from my 30 years in banking. It's also interesting because this book has more text than usual. Despite investing a lot in courses, books, and other self-development tools, it wasn't until I recognized the importance of pattern recognition that things truly started to come together.

A concerning pattern I've observed in too many small businesses is the lack of documentation and processes. Your business should be designed to be scalable, repeatable, and 'franchiseable' (a term I coined). Let me break these down:

Scalable: Your business should be able to scale up effortlessly. This means having the right systems and automation in place, so that when your marketing hits the mark and customers are clamoring for your services, you can maintain a high level of service. According to Salesforce, 86% of consumers say that the experience a company provides is as important as its products or services, emphasizing the need for scalable solutions that don't compromise on customer service.

Repeatable: Consistency is key. Even if you're delivering average results, predictability is crucial. McDonald's, for example, may not serve the world's best burgers, but customers know they can expect a consistent experience. The worst thing you can do is set an expectation higher than you can consistently deliver.

Franchiseable: Your business processes should be so well-documented that if someone like Elon Musk were to buy your business, his team could operate it without your input. Documented procedures not only improve your business but also facilitate the onboarding of new staff or volunteers.

Many business owners keep everything in their head, thinking they're the only ones who can manage it all. This is a bottleneck waiting to happen.

Even as a solopreneur, having your processes documented is critical. If you reach a stage where you can hire a PA or VA, having documented procedures is invaluable. It allows you to delegate effectively and ensures continuity of service.

This topic alone could fill a book. It's why my passion lies in working with businesses that are -6 to 12 months old—I can help them establish the correct systems that will aid in growth and ensure a professional image.

An effective CRM system is pivotal to efficient business systems. Some think they're too small for a CRM, but it's crucial to start from day one. A CRM can accelerate growth and prevent 'data leakage,' where customer information or prospects fall through the cracks.

Despite the myriad of voices on social media claiming they can help you find customers; most startups and side hustlers don't need more customers—they need to improve their conversion rates for the leads they already have. Data from Invesp shows that improving your conversion rate by just 1% can increase your revenues by as much as 50%, underscoring the value of a CRM in capturing and converting leads.

By focusing on these three key aspects—scalability, repeatability, and 'franchiseability'—along with implementing a robust CRM, you're not just running a business; you're cultivating an asset that can grow, adapt, and thrive independently of your constant involvement.

This approach will help you establish a viable business underpinned by the correct KPIs (Key Performance Indicators). You will be able to operate a data-driven business that can either be sold or passed down to future generations. Consequently, you will own a company, not merely a job.

Mic Check: Summarizing The Key Points

This book is designed to be evergreen. As technology advances, the 'in' social media platforms will inevitably change, as will the apps and platforms themselves. These principles are founded on human nature and science, which are unlikely to change anytime soon.

This book is a great standalone resource for startups and side hustlers. It draws from my three decades of experience as a business owner, banker, consultant, and entrepreneur. I've tried to provide the key things you will need to do as a business owner.

There are a lot of good business books out there, and hopefully, you will count this among the useful books that you have read. With that said, this book is also perfect for our in-person or online training.

We conduct in-person sessions both here and in the UK. We always welcome new delegates.

If you would like to attend one of our Business Mastery Courses, please visit www.startupsandsidehustlers.com. It's a great way to expand your network, learn, share, and discover new ways to run a more effective and profitable business.

Digital Marketing and Social Media TermsScaling

In digital marketing, this refers to the ability to increase advertising efforts and reach while maintaining or improving return on investment (ROI) and efficiency. It involves gradually enhancing campaign budgets, expanding to new channels, or targeting wider audiences without sacrificing performance.

Customer Acquisition Cost (CAC)

This is the total cost of acquiring a new customer, including all aspects of marketing and sales divided by the number of new customers acquired. It's a key metric to evaluate the effectiveness of marketing campaigns.

Customer Lifetime Value (CLV)

A prediction of the net profit attributed to the entire future relationship with a customer. Understanding CLV helps businesses develop strategies to acquire new customers and retain existing ones while maintaining profit margins.

Net Promoter Score (NPS)

A metric used to measure customer loyalty and satisfaction by asking customers how likely they are to recommend a company's products or services to others on a scale of 0-10. The scores are used to classify customers into Promoters, Passives, and Detractors.

Friction

Any element of your website or user experience that can cause frustration, delay, or confusion for users, potentially resulting in them leaving the site without converting. Reducing friction is crucial for improving conversion rates.

Conversion Rate Optimization (CRO)

The systematic process of increasing the percentage of website visitors who take a desired action — be that filling out a form, becoming customers, or otherwise. The process involves understanding how users move through your site, what actions they take, and what's stopping them from completing your goals.

Search Engine Optimization (SEO)

The practice of increasing the quantity and quality of traffic to your website through organic search engine results. This involves optimizing your website to rank higher in search engine results pages (SERPs) for targeted keywords.

Content Marketing

A strategic marketing approach focused on creating and distributing valuable, relevant, and consistent content to attract and retain a clearly defined audience — and, ultimately, to drive profitable customer action.

Pay-Per-Click (PPC)

An online advertising model in which an advertiser pays a publisher every time an advertisement link is 'clicked' on. PPC is commonly associated with Google AdWords and Bing Ads.

Social Media Engagement

A measure of how people are interacting with a company's social media accounts and content. This can include metrics like comments, likes, shares, and retweets, which are indicators of your brand's presence and popularity on social media platforms.

A quick note, when it comes to social media for business purposes, be a producer and not a consumer. It is easy to spend hours scrolling through posts and images. Social media is designed to be addictive.

You should spend 10 - 20 minutes a day producing content for social media. This time should be based on a very clear strategy. This should be productive time designed to fill your funnels or connect with your top 50.

Summary

1. Mastering the Plan is Vital for Success

A well-defined business plan is crucial, serving as a roadmap to guide startups and side hustlers through the entrepreneurial landscape. Consistently reviewing and adapting the business plan is necessary to navigate the ever-evolving market conditions and ensure long-term success.

2. Building a Strong Network is Priceless

Networking should be viewed as a strategic component of business growth, not a sporadic activity. Establishing genuine connections can lead to opportunities beyond immediate transactions. It's about creating value for others and leveraging the law of reciprocity.

3. Your Website is Your Best Employee

Consider your website an integral part of your team. It works tirelessly, assisting with sales, customer service, and data collection. Aligning your website with your CRM and sales funnels can transform it into a powerful tool for growth.

4. Sales Funnels are the Engine of Your Sales Machine

A deep understanding and implementation of effective sales funnels can significantly boost conversion rates and the average sale amount. A well-structured sales funnel guides customers smoothly from interest to purchase, maximizing the return on advertising spend.

5. Understanding Customer Psychology Drives Conversions

Recognizing the emotional, logical, and fear-based factors that influence buying decisions is key. Crafting sales pitches and marketing strategies that address these aspects can improve conversion rates. Align your value proposition with the customer's desires and pain points for better results.

We've revisited the essential elements that form the foundation of a successful entrepreneurial venture. From meticulously crafting a business plan to the nuanced art of networking, the synergy of an efficient website, the strategic deployment of sales funnels, and a deep understanding of customer psychology, these pillars support a robust and dynamic business structure. Moving forward, keep these key points at the forefront of your strategy, allowing them to guide you to a rhythm of success that resonates with your vision and values.

Smart actions

1. Business Plan Development & Review

Specific: Create a comprehensive business plan that outlines the startup's vision, mission, objectives, strategies, and a detailed financial plan.

Measurable: Include specific financial targets and milestones for product development, marketing, sales, and customer acquisition.

Achievable: Ensure the plan is realistic, considering current resources and market conditions.

Relevant: The plan should align with the long-term goals of the business and the current market needs.

Time-bound: Complete the initial draft within 1 month and set bimonthly reviews for adapting the plan.

2. Strategic Networking

Specific: Actively engage with industry leaders, potential clients, and business peers through networking events and social media platforms.

Measurable: Aim to establish connections with at least 5 new contacts per month and follow up with them.

Achievable: Attend at least two networking events or online webinars each month.

Relevant: Networking should lead to potential business opportunities, partnerships, or mentorship.

Time-bound: Review networking goals and outcomes quarterly.

3. Website Optimization

Specific: Enhance the website to automate sales, customer service, and data collection processes.

Measurable: Implement CRM integration and establish metrics for user engagement and conversion rates.

Achievable: Assign this task to a web developer or use website optimization tools.

Relevant: A functional website can serve as a 24/7 salesperson for the business.

Time-bound: Complete the website updates and integration within 3 months.

4. Sales Funnel Efficiency

Specific: Design and implement a multi-stage sales funnel tailored to the business's customer journey.

Measurable: Track conversion rates at each stage of the funnel and work towards a set improvement percentage.

Achievable: Use marketing automation tools to create and manage the sales funnel.

Relevant: Effective sales funnels are critical for converting leads into customers.

Time-bound: Develop and test the sales funnel over a 6-month period.

5. Customer Psychology Analysis

Specific: Conduct market research to understand customer behavior and tailor marketing and sales strategies accordingly.

Measurable: Use customer feedback and sales data to measure the impact of tailored strategies on conversion rates.

Achievable: Gather data through surveys, focus groups, and sales analytics.

Relevant: Understanding customer psychology is essential for improving sales effectiveness.

Time-bound: Complete initial customer psychology analysis within 4 months and apply findings to sales strategies.

6. Overall Strategic Implementation:

Specific: Integrate the five key points into the business's strategic plan.

Measurable: Review business performance against the strategic plan's targets.

Achievable: Assign responsibilities to team members for each key area.

Relevant: Each element is designed to support the business's growth and success.

Time-bound: Implement the strategic plan over the course of a year with quarterly reviews and adjustments.

Remember, the key to a successful SMART action plan is regular review and adaptability to change.

Productivity Hacks

Here are 10 productivity hacks for your Startup or Side Hustle

Prepare Your Day at Night: Plan your next day the night before. This could include making a to-do list, laying out clothes, meal prepping, or even a moment of meditation to visualize your goals.

Use a Task Timer: Implement a task timer to break tasks into timed intervals, helping you focus and understand how long tasks take. Our WC Portal CRM has a built in timer.

Exercise Regularly: Regular exercise helps keep you active, reduces stress, and improves sleep quality, all of which are crucial for productivity.

Put Your Phone Away: During focused work periods, keep your smartphone out of sight to minimize distractions. This is easier if you have a dedicated business phone number, which we strongly recommend.

End Your Day with a Review: Spend a few moments at the end of each day reviewing what went well, what was challenging, and areas for improvement.

Delegate Tasks: Know when to delegate and outsource tasks to focus on more critical aspects of your business. This could include getting a virtual assistant.

Set Goals and Track Progress: Set SMART goals and break them down into actionable items. Regularly review and track your progress towards these goals. This book talks a lot about S.M.A.R.T goals and give some good examples of goals that you can set for your business..

Have separate business number: Get a separate business number. This could mean getting a "business" sim card to put in a dual sim phone. Goaddy also has a product called SmartLine.

Schedule Time for Self-Care: Make self-care a part of your routine to avoid burnout. This can include reading, exercising, journaling, or praying.

Implementing these hacks can lead to a more organized, efficient, and balanced work-life, enhancing productivity for Startups and Side Hustlers.

Bark.com: Bark.com is a web-based services marketplace that connects customers with professional service providers. It operates in various countries and covers over 800 different service categories. The platform allows clients in need of professional help to send requests to freelancers, ensuring they have the relevant skills and are from a nearby location.

I use Bark to test my lead funnels. I set a very specific profile for the type of clients that I want. I set aside some business development time and wait for leads to come in. I only purchase leads that have not been contacted by any other providers. I immediately call, text and email, then I put them in my CRM drip feed. This increases the possibility of me securing some kind of sale and prevents data leakage.

Freelancer.com: A popular platform with over 50 million users, offering a wide range of freelance categories. It operates on a bidding system, where freelancers compete by submitting proposals for projects.

PeoplePerHour.com: Focuses on small to medium-sized projects. Freelancers can create "hourlies" for fixed-price services. The platform is known for its AI-driven project matching and user-friendly interface.

Each of these platforms has its own unique features and specialties, catering to different needs and preferences of freelancers and clients.

ChatGPT Business Prompts

A few really good prompts just in case you don't have ChatGPT Prompts for Startups and Side Huslers.

Prompt for Social Media Strategy:

Prompt: "Create a 6-month social media marketing plan for [business type], including content themes, posting frequency, and engagement tactics."

Use Case: Assists in developing a structured and effective social media strategy to enhance online presence and engagement.

Prompt for Email Marketing Campaign:

Prompt: "Design an email marketing campaign for [product/service], focusing on content, layout, and call-to-action for maximizing conversions."

Use Case: Useful for crafting targeted email campaigns to boost sales or brand awareness.

Thank you for taking the time to read this book. It would be great to hear about your progress. You can connect with me on Linkedin

We are building a community of like-minded business professionals. Join our UK Whatsapp group.

As I approached my 50th birthday a few years back I took stock of my life. I reviewed my bucket list. One of my goals was to write a book. At the time I didn't think that less than 3-years later I would have 8 books written and 4 published. If you have ever thought about writing a book I encourage you to get started. We have developed a very useful GPT that will help you with all of the technical stuff. **Here it is.**

When you are ready to format your book and generate 2d/3d mock-ups there is a great tool. It's the same one that we use. Check it out here

Get More YouTube Subscribers Make your YouTube Channel Go Viral!
Sprizzy promotes your channel with YouTube Ads to get subscribers quickly
and easily.

Sprizzy promotes your videos across the YouTube ads platform, reaching
viewers watching videos just like yours. Our YouTube Ads will expose your
videos to the masses and quickly gain you new subscribers.

Keep track of all of our in-person and online events. We would love to meet you in person.

Astor Business Centers, Inc. stands as the premier destination for business solutions, offering a comprehensive suite of services tailored for entrepreneurs. We facilitate connections between business owners and a wide array of essential resources, including people, products, and services.

Leveraging our expansive networks across the US and UK, we are uniquely positioned to link businesses with a diverse global audience. Our commitment to affordability and transparency sets us apart. For more details, reach out to us at (832) 617-7959 in the US or 0203 633-6682 in the UK, or schedule a meeting to discover how we can assist in your business growth.

BUSINESS
MASTERY
FOR STARTUPS AND
SIDE HUSTLERS

Planning, launching and
running a business
on a budget

Anthony Lindsay - CeMaP, CeReR